THE BOOK OF
IRISH LEGENDS

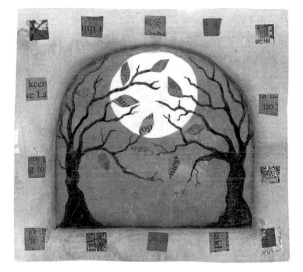

THE BOOK OF
IRISH LEGENDS

IAIN ZACZEK

ILLUSTRATED BY EMMA GARNER

CICO BOOKS

London

Published by Cico Books (formerly Cima Books)
32 Great Sutton Street, London EC1V 0NB

Copyright © Cico Books 2001
Text copyright © Iain Zaczek 2001

10 9 8 7 6 5 4 3 2 1

ISBN 1 903116 39 2

Designed by David Fordham

Illustrations by Emma Garner

Printed and bound in Portugal by Printer Portuguesa

Contents

INTRODUCTION

OVER THE CENTURIES, the Irish have gained an enviable reputation for their unsurpassed gifts as storytellers. In part, this has been made possible by the unique store of tales and legends at their disposal. This marvelous repertoire dates back to the very roots of Irish civilization and includes a remarkable variety of themes, ranging from noble kings and warrior-heroes to shape-shifting fairies and evil magicians.

The storytelling tradition was developed by the Celts who settled in Ireland around the 3rd century BC. They devised a colorful series of legends to illustrate the qualities of their sizeable pantheon of gods. These mythical stories were transmitted orally from generation to generation, evolving over the course of many centuries. During the Middle Ages, they were written down and preserved by Christian scribes. Because of the piecemeal way that they were collected, however, these legends do not form a single, coherent narrative. Instead, they are usually grouped into story cycles, revolving around a central character. The most important of these are the Ulster Cycle and the Fionn, or Fenian, Cycle.

The Ulster Cycle contains the most ancient tales and deals with the exploits of Cú Chulainn, the champion of Ulster, who wages war single-handedly against the forces of Connacht. This conflict is described in an epic story, *The Cattle Raid of Cooley*, which concerns the theft of a magical bull. The episode in this volume (p.98) is drawn from the lengthy Cooley narrative and typifies its blend of savagery and magic. Cú Chulainn is classified as a mortal, but he and his principal enemies have superhuman powers and, in the earliest forms of the legend, were probably deities. The setting of the tales, however, has an authentic, historical flavor. Indeed, experts have claimed that the Ulster Cycle presents a vivid picture of Irish military life in the 1st century BC.

The Fionn Cycle dates from the 3rd century AD and manifests a very different spirit. The earlier emphasis on superhuman feats and individuality is replaced by a greater concern for comradeship and nobility. The eponymous hero is Fionn mac Cumhaill, a Leinster chieftain who founded a warrior-band called the Fianna. The members of this elite group were noted for their skill at hunting and poetry, though their principal function was to defend Ireland against a range of enemies, both human and supernatural. In many eyes, they have been seen as a Celtic prototype for the Arthurian Knights of the Round Table.

The Fenian tales remained popular in Ireland long after the coming of Christianity. They evolved considerably and as a result, some inconsistencies can be found. There is a world of difference, for example, between the noble depiction of Fionn in *The Chase of Slieve Gullion* and the bitter, vindictive figure portrayed in *The Death of Diarmaid*. Similarly, there was a growing shift of interest away from the central character. Other members of the Fianna, such as Diarmaid, Oisin, and Cailte, became the focus of their own cycles. This is particularly true of Oisin, whose popularity eventually eclipsed that of Fionn. During the Middle Ages the tales of his visit to the Otherworld and his meetings with St. Patrick were widely circulated. He became the focal point of the Celtic revival, which swept across Europe in the early 19th century.

There is also a wide selection of Irish stories which are grouped together by theme rather than character, notably the Echtrae ("Adventures"), which flourished during the medieval era. The majority of these describe a hero's journey to the Otherworld. Usually he is lured away by a beautiful maiden or mysterious warrior, and is dazzled by the marvels he encounters. The traveler may return with some priceless memento, but all too often the experience costs him his life. *Connla and the Fairy Maiden* and *Cormac and the Fairy Branch* are fine examples.

Another group, the "Voyages" or Imrama (literally "Rowings") is closely affiliated to the Echtrae. They feature expeditions to the Otherworld, but the emphasis is on the journey, rather than the supernatural destination. There has been much speculation about the source of these Imrama, with some theorists arguing that they were based on the reports of genuine Irish seafarers. Others believe that they were inspired by classical texts, or by the Arthurian tales of the quest for the Holy Grail.

The Voyage of Maeldun is one of the oldest surviving examples of this genre, with most authorities agreeing that it dates from the 8th century. It may also be one of the most influential tales, since it is invariably cited as a key source for *The Voyage of Saint Brendan*, a landmark 10th-century text recounting the apocryphal travels of St. Brendan of Clonfert (d.577), which became a bestseller and was translated into several European languages.

Some elements from the ancient legends were incorporated into popular Irish folk-tales. For modern readers, the best-known anthologies are probably those compiled by Douglas Hyde (*Beside the Fire*, 1890) and W.B. Yeats (*Fairy and Folk-Tales of the Irish Peasantry*, 1888). However, the leading pioneer in this field was Thomas Crofton Croker (1798–1854). His *Fairy Legends and Traditions of the South of Ireland* first appeared in 1823, and was greatly admired by both Sir Walter Scott and Jacob Grimm. Croker's book described a fascinating array of fairy spirits and monsters, among them the merrow, the cluricaune, and the banshee. The most notable, however, was the pooka, a devilish creature that preyed upon unsuspecting mortals. Stories about this mischievous fairy had been popular for centuries, and have often been cited as a source for the character of Puck, in Shakespeare's play *A Midsummer Night's Dream*.

THE LEGENDS
AND
FAIRY TALES

Connla and the Fairy Maiden

No man brought greater glory to Ireland than Conn of the Hundred Battles, the noble king who ruled at Tara. Together with his son, Connla the Red, he mounted a daily patrol at the high places in his kingdom, keeping watch in case the fairy people rose from their mounds and laid claim to Ireland.

All went well until one day, when the two men were walking with their retinue on the sacred hill of Ushnagh. As they looked out across the plain, Connla espied a beautiful maiden riding toward them. She wore the strangest clothing, however, which made him think that she came from a distant country.

"Where are you from, fair maid?" he asked, as she drew near.

"I come from Tír na mBeo," she replied, "the Land of the Living, where none grow sick and none grow old. We have no wars, no crimes, no quarrels. Instead, we spend all our time in feasting and lovemaking."

These words caused great amazement among Conn and his people, for although they could hear the lady's speech quite plainly, she remained completely invisible to them. Connla alone could see her, and the honey in her voice held him in thrall. This worried the king, so he turned to his son and asked him what he saw.

But the fairy woman answered in his stead: "Connla sees a high-born lady, who will never have wrinkles and will never die. Come with

me now, fair prince, and I will make you lord of my domain. You shall reign forever in Fairyland, where nothing will ever cause you sorrow or pain."

Now Conn was full of fear for his son. Swiftly, he called Coran the Druid to his side, imploring him to use his powers to nullify the fairy's enchantment. Obediently, the druid began to recite his magical verses, drowning out the beguiling words of the woman. As he did so, the fairy started to fade out of Connla's sight, though she threw him an apple as she left.

Throughout the following month, Connla kept this apple with him, refusing all other food and drink. And, though he ate freely of the apple, yet it remained whole and perfect. All the while, the youth was listless and sad, thinking of nothing else but the woman in his vision.

After a month, Conn and Connla strolled together again, by the shores of Arcomin. As they walked, the fairy maid returned, riding in a crystal ship. "Connla," she called out, "your homeland may be wonderful, but old age and death await you, if you linger here. Come with me now, and I will give you life eternal."

Hearing these words, Conn beckoned for his druid, but the woman forestalled him. "Too late, noble king, for the prince has eaten of my apple, and its power will scatter the druid's spells on his lips. Come,

Connla, join me now and we will sail to a faraway land in the golden west; a land of sweetness and pleasure."

To the king's dismay, Connla did her bidding and stepped into her crystal curragh. Then they glided away, heading toward the setting sun. Conn and his people gazed sadly after them, until they disappeared from view. And no one can tell whether Connla found his realm of promise and eternal youth, for he was never seen again in his native land.

THE VOYAGE OF
MAELDUN

THE START OF THE VOYAGE

THERE WAS ONCE A valiant warrior named Ailill Ochair Aga, chieftain of the Owenaght tribe. His life was glorious but brief, for a band of marauders came to his land and plundered it mercilessly. Ailill took refuge in a nearby church, but the villains followed him there and slew him, burning the building to the ground.

The Owenaght mourned for their dead leader, none more so than the nun who was carrying his child. Three months later, she gave birth to a son and named him Maeldun. Then, wishing to conceal the illegitimacy of his birth, she took him to the queen of a neighboring land and begged her to raise the child as her own. This noble lady took pity on her and agreed to the request.

So Maeldun was raised in a royal household, with all the honor and care that befitted a prince. In time, he proved himself worthy of these attentions, for he grew to excel in every field. No youth was more skilled at mastering a horse, or handling a sword, or outwitting an opponent at chess. But these very qualities were to be the source of many woes, for they fired the jealousy of his foster brothers. One of these complained loudly about the shame of competing with a mere changeling, whose origins were so uncertain.

Upon hearing this, Maeldun went immediately to the queen and implored her to tell him the true nature of his birth. She eventually

agreed, though she felt it would bring the youth little but sorrow. Thus
Maeldun came to learn of the cruel fate of Ailill. The story filled his
heart with anger and he vowed to hunt down the pirates, even if it
meant searching every corner of the oceans. Straight away, he
consulted with Corcomroe the Druid, who showed him the way to
build a magical, triple-hide curragh, large enough to hold seventeen
men. Then, after receiving the wise man's blessing, he set off on his
perilous quest.

The Palace of the Little Cat

Maeldun and his companions sailed westwards for many days, and it was not long before they found themselves in uncharted waters. By now, their store of food and drink was almost exhausted, and it seemed as if their voyage would end before it had truly begun.

Then, on the seventeenth day, one of the sailors sighted land. Gratefully, the party went ashore to look for provisions and make enquiries about the raiders. In this last respect, their search proved fruitless, for the island appeared to be uninhabited. All they could find was a single building, a gleaming white palace. Maeldun entered this with his companions, proceeding toward a large, central chamber.

There, they witnessed a sight that rendered them speechless. The room was a glittering treasure-store. Cordoned off behind a row of four stone columns, piles of golden torcs, silver rings, and jeweled brooches lay heaped upon the floor. Amazingly, there was no one there to guard these riches. Indeed, the only living creature in the place was a tiny, white cat, which was amusing itself by leaping from one column to the next. As the men walked into the room, the cat looked across at them for a moment, but soon lost interest and returned to its play.

Before they could examine these treasures more closely, one of Maeldun's followers noticed something else. "Look!" he said, pointing to the far end of the room. There, on a long trestle table, a magnificent

feast awaited them. There was roast ox and pork, fruit of every kind and, beside the table, a fountain where ale and wine flowed freely. The famished sailors needed no further invitation. Casting caution aside, they rushed to the table and gorged themselves on the food. Then, once they had eaten their fill, they fell into a deep, satisfied sleep.

Next day, Maeldun instructed his companions to gather up any remaining food, so that they could take it back to their vessel.

"What about this treasure?" asked one of the men. "Should we bring it too?"

"By no means," replied Maeldun. "We have feasted well. Let us be grateful for that. Besides, it seems suspicious to me that such jewels should be left unguarded. Who knows what curse may hang over them."

All the mariners obeyed these orders, with one exception. The youngest of the crew was unimpressed by Maeldun's words of wisdom

and, as they were leaving the palace, he slipped a large, golden torc into his coat. No one noticed, apart from the little white cat, which followed him out of the building. It trailed behind him for a few moments, until suddenly it leaped up at the thief, its body glowing like a flaming arrow. In an instant, it had passed right through the sailor, reducing him to a heap of ashes. Then, resuming its original color, it turned around and loped back into the palace.

The voyagers were shocked by this and some of them wanted to attack the cat, but Maeldun held them back. Instead, he picked up the torc and returned it to its rightful place, in the treasure chamber. The cat appeared pleased with this and licked his hand. Then Maeldun gave orders that their comrade's ashes should be gathered up and cast into the sea. After this, they continued on their way, silently mourning the loss of their companion.

The Island of Black and White

THREE DAYS LATER, they arrived at another island. Here, there was a curious partition, a long brass wall, which stretched as far as the eye could see. Large numbers of sheep roamed freely on either side of the fence, though they appeared to belong to different flocks. For on one side, the sheep had fleecy white coats, while on the other they were uniformly black.

The sheep were tended by a gigantic man, who was leaning against the wall. From time to time, he lifted up a beast and placed it on the opposite side of the barrier. When he transferred a black sheep in this manner, its coat would immediately become white. Similarly, when he moved a white sheep to the other section, its coat turned black.

The voyagers were astounded by this strange phenomenon and decided to try an experiment. They threw a piece of driftwood toward the island, and watched with fascination as the colors were bleached out of it, when it reached the shore. Then they pulled it back to their curragh with a hook and cast it on the other side. Now, in an instant, the wood became jet black.

After this, Maeldun gave orders that they should continue their voyage, without setting foot on the island. So the boat departed, with the sailors still marveling at the wonders they had seen.

The Isle of Weeping

IT WAS NOT LONG before Maeldun and his companions happened upon another island. This proved to be the most populous of all the places they had visited. For, as they drew near to the shore, they could see a great multitude of people, walking back and forth. They were dressed entirely in black, and all of them appeared to be weeping and wringing their hands. Indeed, their grief was so great that they did not even look up, as the mariners landed their craft.

"Surely some terrible tragedy must have occurred here," said Maeldun. "Nevertheless, we must try and question the islanders, to see if they have any news of my father's murderers."

One of Maeldun's foster brothers volunteered to carry out this task and, without further ado, he leaped out of the curragh and went ashore. There, he approached the nearest of the mourners and engaged him in conversation.

The voyagers watched this discussion from afar, patiently awaiting Maeldun's order to disembark. Their eagerness turned to concern, however, as their companion's mission appeared to go wrong. For, instead of returning to the boat to report his findings, the sailor became more and more engrossed in his conversation. As he did so, his face gradually took on a sorrowful expression. Soon, tears were rolling down his cheeks and he had started to pace up and down, exactly like the other islanders. The mariners called out to their friend, asking what was amiss, but he paid no attention to them. His whole being, it seemed, was consumed by grief.

Several of the voyagers wanted to leap ashore immediately and rescue their colleague, but Maeldun advised caution. He selected two strong men for the task, instructing them to bind their mantles tightly around their ears and mouths. He also stressed that they should take care not to communicate with anyone on the island, not even their colleague, and that they should bring him back by force if necessary.

The pair did as they were told. Once ashore, they headed straight for their companion, looking neither to the left nor the right. Then, they grabbed hold of his arms and began to drag him back to the boat. As Maeldun had foreseen, his foster brother did not come willingly. He struggled violently with the men, shouting abuse at them, but they could not hear his words, because of the bindings over their ears. The other mourners, meanwhile, continued with their weeping and made no attempt to interfere.

Once the man was aboard, he came to his senses. Maeldun questioned him about the reason for his actions, but the fellow had no memory of events upon the island. He only knew that, once he had spoken with the mourner, he was filled with an overpowering compulsion to stay and join him. This compulsion had been so strong that, but for the help of his friends, he felt sure that he would have remained there for the rest of his days.

After hearing this account, the voyagers made haste to depart, grateful that they had escaped from the dangers of this curious island.

THE PALACE OF THE CRYSTAL BRIDGE

MAELDUN AND HIS COMPANIONS doubted if they would ever come upon a stranger place than the Isle of Weeping, but events would soon prove them wrong. For, within a few days, they landed at an even more outlandish spot, in the farthest corner of the Western Sea.

After a brief patrol, it seemed that the only building of note was an imposing fortress. The entrance to this stronghold was made of bronze and it was decked out with several rows of tiny, silver bells. The only access to it, however, lay across a long, crystal bridge, which spanned a yawning chasm. Toward the far end of the bridge, there was also a fountain, full of clear, running water.

Maeldun and his followers tried to approach the stronghold by this means but, as soon as they set foot on the bridge, an unseen force lifted them up and hurled them on their backs. After several failed attempts, they decided to conceal themselves and await the arrival of the fort's inhabitants. Eventually, their hopes were fulfilled, as a beautiful young woman emerged from the building, carrying a pail. At the edge of the bridge, she moved a little crystal slab, which enabled her to proceed to the fountain. There, she filled up her pail, before returning to the stronghold.

Now that the way was open, the sailors hurried across the bridge and knocked on the door. This set the bells ringing, however, and they played a melody so sweet that it lulled the voyagers into a deep sleep.

They remained in this state until the following morning, when the same maid came out of the fort, to fetch water from the fountain. As she returned, she remarked: "Wake up, noble Maeldun. Is this an example to set your followers?" Her words roused the men from their slumbers but, before they had fully revived, she vanished inside the stronghold once more. The sailors immediately called out to her and banged on the door, but this only had the effect of setting off the bewitching melody of the bells. As a result, the voyagers were soon fast asleep again.

The same thing happened for three consecutive mornings, during which time Maeldun and his men progressed no further than the palace door. On the fourth day, however, the woman emerged from the stronghold without her pail. This time, she roused the voyagers with the words: "Hail, noble Maeldun. My love and blessings upon you and your companions." The mariners stirred sleepily and, as soon as they opened their eyes, they were amazed at the lady's appearance. For, now the woman was attired like a queen. She wore a resplendent gown, with a white mantle on her shoulders and a golden circlet on her brow.

Then she welcomed each of the sailors by name and led them inside the stronghold. There, they were ushered into a large banqueting chamber, where they made themselves comfortable on luxurious couches. Next, she brought forth meat and drink out of her pail, the

same pail that she had carried to the fountain. This single vessel provided food enough to satisfy the entire company. And, whatever kind of food or drink each seaman most desired, that was the taste of the goods in her pail.

Now the voyagers began to discuss amongst themselves the great merits of this woman, believing that she would make a worthy wife for their leader. They broached this matter with Maeldun, offering to make a formal approach to the lady on his behalf, and he was all agreement. While they had been eating, however, the woman had slipped out of their presence and was nowhere to be found. The sailors searched the entire palace, but there was no sign of her. So, they decided to sleep that night on the couches and hope that she would return on the morrow.

Next morning, the voyagers' wishes were fulfilled, when the lady arrived with her pail, ready to feed them. After they had eaten their fill, they raised the question of marriage, reciting the praises of their leader. She listened attentively, before replying: "I am well aware of the virtues of noble Maeldun, for the details of your quest were prophesied here. Nevertheless, I cannot grant your request, for I am forbidden to marry with any son of man." So saying she departed, before the mariners could ask for any further explanation.

Maeldun's companions were unhappy with this response, and decided to make another attempt to bring about the match. Accordingly, they decided to stay for a further night in the palace and press their suit in the morning.

So, on the following day, when the maiden returned with her pail, the sailors refused to touch a morsel of food, until they had discussed the matter again. With honeyed words, they redoubled their praises of Maeldun and urged the woman to return with them to their homeland. She listened to their words and gave the following answer: "I confess, my lords, I am greatly impressed by the love and loyalty that you show toward your leader. Grant me a little time, however, before I make my reply. For now, feast yourselves on the dainties in this vessel and sleep here tonight on these couches. Tomorrow, I will give you my answer."

The mariners were well pleased with this promising response and readily agreed to the lady's requests. They ate heartily from the food in the pail and slept for a third night in the palace. On the following morning, however, they received a tremendous shock. For, when they awoke, they found themselves back on their curragh, in the middle of the open sea. And, though they searched far and wide, they never managed to discover the slightest trace of the island with the palace of the crystal bridge.

The Isle of Speaking Birds

ONE NIGHT, not long after this, the mariners were roused from their slumbers by a confused babble of voices. It sounded as if the noise came from a great multitude of people, all speaking at the same time, though one of the sailors thought that it resembled a chorus of psalms.

When dawn broke, the sailors began to row in the direction of the sound. For a day and a night they rowed without rest, until finally an island came into view. As they drew nearer, the clamor of the voices

grew louder still, as if an army of men was shouting at each other. This made no sense, however, for it gradually became clear that the island was nothing more than a single pinnacle of rock. No humans were visible on this crag. Instead, the stone was covered with a great host of birds. These were of every breed and hue – some brown, some black, some speckled – but the oddest thing about them was that each one spoke with a human voice.

The sailors listened intently to these voices, but it was impossible to understand a word of what was being said, since all the birds were talking at the same time. Because of this, there seemed little point in trying to question the creatures. Besides, one of the mariners had spotted another island in the distance, so Maeldun gave orders that they should row toward this instead.

THE HERMIT

As THE VOYAGERS came within reach of the second island, they could see that this too was inhabited by scores of birds. Fortunately, the silhouette of a human being was also visible. On closer inspection, this turned out to be a frail, old man. His flesh was pale and wrinkled, and every inch of his body was covered in long, white hair.

The mariners were eager to know what had brought the ancient one to this place, but they were surprised by his reply.

"I am an Irishman, my friends. Many years ago, I set out from my native land on a pilgrimage. I had not gone very far, however, when my curragh began to sink. Naturally I returned to the shore, but when I stepped out into the shallow water, a clod of earth floated up to the surface, beneath my feet, and carried me away. It became my sailing craft, bringing me to this spot, and now it is my home. For, with God's assistance, that clod of earth has grown into this island."

The voyagers were amazed at this story, wondering how the old man had survived. Then the hermit told them that the Lord had caused a spring of ale to well up on the island, which served him for drink, while a tame otter brought him salmon from the sea. "As for the birds," he continued, "those are the souls of my children and my relatives, just as the birds on the neighboring isle are the souls of other Irish men and women. And all of us will abide here together until the end of the world, for we are all awaiting the Day of Judgment."

Then the hermit offered the mariners his hospitality, feeding them on salmon and ale. After they had feasted well, Maeldun quizzed him about the raiders who had slain his father. At this, the old man grew pensive. "I know of the men you mention and can easily help you find them, but you must make me a promise."

"Name it," said Maeldun.

"If I direct you to your goal, you must swear to me that you will neither kill nor take revenge on the men in any way. For God has protected you in your journey, preserving you from dangers that might easily have brought you to your doom. So, in recompense for His bounty, you must show forgiveness and be reconciled with your enemy."

This was a hard thing to ask of Maeldun and his companions, after all the perils that they had faced. But they realized that God had guided them throughout their quest, and was speaking to them now through this hermit. So they followed his instructions and travelled to the isle, where the pirates were quartered. There, they were reconciled, with each man recounting his adventures. Then, after they had feasted and rested, they returned to their homeland, where they lived together as brothers.

41

How Diarmaid got his Love-Spot

In ancient times, when Cormac mac Airt ruled at Tara, there was a noble band of warriors named the Fianna, who performed great deeds in Ireland. Fionn mac Cumhaill was their leader and, of all his followers, the most valued was Diarmaid. No man could wield a sword with greater force; no man was keener in the hunt; and no man had such charms to woo the ladies.

It happened one day that the men of the Fianna went out hunting, and Diarmaid was among their number. From sunrise to sunset, they coursed across the slopes of Mount Muisire looking for game, but not a single living creature crossed their path. As darkness fell, the party split up, and every man began to look for food and shelter. During this search, Diarmaid and three companions – Goll, Conan and Oscar – came upon a mean hovel, nestling at the foot of the hill.

"Let us ride on," urged Conan, eyeing the cottage scornfully, "for there is little chance of us finding a decent meal at such a place as this."

"You are too hasty," replied Diarmaid. "Besides, the hour grows late, and we are all hungry and tired."

So saying, he dismounted and went to knock upon the door. An aged, silver-haired man opened it and beckoned the hunters in, as if they were old friends whom he had been expecting. Inside, the dwelling seemed surprisingly large. The four comrades were ushered into a spacious room, where a sheep was tethered to a wall and a cat dozed lazily by the open fire.

The old man called out and, from another room, a beautiful young woman entered bearing dishes of food. Hungrily the hunters sat down, anxious to begin their meal. Before they had tasted a single morsel, however, the sheep broke free of its rope and clambered onto the table, scattering food everywhere.

Uttering an impatient oath, Conan rose from his place and laid his hands upon the beast, meaning to tie it up again. But the animal would not budge. Instead, it shook itself with such ferocity that Conan was flung back and tumbled to the floor. From his seat in the corner, the old man looked on with amusement, but said nothing.

Now Goll arose and set his hands upon the animal's back. Once again, however, the sheep proved a match for the warrior. Nothing Goll did would make it shift its position until, with a flick of its shoulders, it hurled the man away. Then it was Oscar's turn, but he fared no better than his companions and soon ended up on the floor.

Finally, Diarmaid tried his strength against the beast. Crouching low, he placed his weight against the flanks of the sheep, trying to throw it off balance. For a moment, it seemed that he would be successful. The animal stumbled and toppled off the table. The sudden momentum also

sent Diarmaid sprawling, however, and quick as a flash, the sheep
turned around and stepped triumphantly onto his chest. Diarmaid tried
to move, but the animal's weight was overpowering and he was trapped.

Now the old man laughed out loud. "Well, men of the Fianna, is
that the best you can do?" So saying, he called out to his cat. It stirred
from its place by the fire and walked across to the sheep. Then,
nudging it with its head, it pushed the beast back to its position by the
wall. There it remained, all meek and docile.

The men of the Fianna returned to the table and looked at their
food. They could have continued eating but, such was their shame,
their appetites had fled. Seeing this, the old man cajoled them. "Eat,
friends, for you have done better than you imagine. That sheep carries
the strength of the whole world and you have wrestled with it bravely,
but only death can overcome it. And that," he said, pointing at the cat,

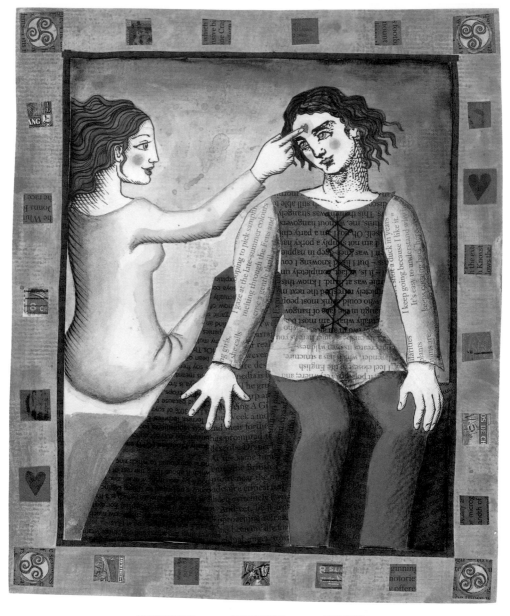

46

"is Death". This revelation cheered the huntsmen and they began to eat again, feasting until their bellies were full.

Once they had finished, the young woman showed them to the place where they could sleep. Then she lay down herself in the same room, and her beauty was so radiant that it seemed to cast a glow upon the walls. For, though the men did not realize it, she was the spirit of Youth.

It did not take long before Conan rose up from his bed and walked across to her. But she rejected him, saying: "Go back to your bed, Conan. I belonged to you once, but I can never be yours again." These words baffled the warrior, but he did as he was told and returned to his couch.

Then Goll stood up, hoping to succeed where his companion had failed. But the maid sent him away, using exactly the same words. Oscar, too, suffered a similar fate, though this did not deter Diarmaid from trying his luck. He approached the woman tentatively, half expecting to be repulsed. As she gazed at the fairness of his face, however, her resolve wavered and she said: "O Diarmaid, I once belonged to you too, and can never be yours again. But come closer, and I will give you a sign of my favor." Then she touched his forehead, and her finger left a mark upon his brow. This mark was a love-spot and, for as long as Diarmaid lived, no woman could look on it without falling in love with him.

Cormac and the Fairy Branch

Wᴴɪʟᴇ Fɪᴏɴɴ ᴍᴀᴄ Cᴜᴍʜᴀɪʟʟ was performing his most valiant deeds, Cormac mac Airt ruled as the high king of Ireland. One day, as he strolled alone outside the ramparts, he saw a tall youth walking toward him holding a silver branch, adorned with nine blood-red apples.

Now this marvelous object was a fairy branch. Whenever it was shaken, the apples would produce an enchanting melody which could soothe the cares of those within earshot. Cormac determinedly asked the youth if he would sell his glittering treasure. "Willingly," the youth replied, "provided you swear to me that you will meet my price." Cormac agreed, confident that the purchase was well within the scope of his kingly riches. The youth gave him the branch, and departed.

At the end of the year, the stranger returned. Yet Cormac's joy at his acquisition turned to sorrow when the youth named his price. "I would have three boons of you," he said, "and the first is that you give me your daughter, Ailbe." With a heavy heart, Cormac agreed, for he had given his word. As the youth departed with the girl there was great lamentation amongst his people, so Cormac shook his branch. Instantly they were soothed, and they fell into a contented slumber.

A month later, the stranger came for his second gift. This time, he took away Carpre, the king's only son. Once again, Cormac's followers wept until he relieved their distress by shaking his fairy branch.

49

After a further thirty days, the youth made his final appearance at court and demanded Ethne, his wife. The king consented, watching with deep regret as his beloved was taken off by the stranger.

When he could bear his torment no longer, Cormac set out in search of his family. He had not gone far when a strange mist descended and, when he emerged, he found himself on an immense plain. Traveling on, he came upon a host of fairy horsemen trying to thatch a beautiful palace with the wings of white birds. Always, as their job neared completion, a mystic wind arose and blew away the feathers.

Next, the king came upon a young man kindling a fire. The youth hauled logs and timbers to the flames, but they burned with such speed that each time he returned, the blaze had dwindled to a heap of embers.

Cormac journeyed on until he reached an even more impressive palace. In its courtyard was a huge, sparkling fountain, with five streams flowing from it. Above were nine hazel trees, spreading their branches above the water. Each was laden with purple nuts, which fell into the streams and were eaten by large salmon.

Cormac was then greeted by a striking couple. They were tall and fair, with garments that were all the colors of the world. They bade him join them in a meal, and presently a quartered pig was brought in and placed in a cooking pot. Cormac was confused, for there was no fire.

"Do not be concerned" said the man, "this cauldron has magical properties. Every time a truth is told, a portion of meat will be cooked.

"I have but a single pig," he continued, "but it will suffice to feed me until the end of my days. For, after I have boiled it in this cauldron, I return the animal's bones to its sty and, the following morning, it is alive." Then the man lifted a piece of pork from the cauldron and ate it. To Cormac's amazement, the meat was cooked.

Next, the woman spoke. "I have seven sheep and seven cows. And the milk from my cattle can quench the thirst of all the people living on this

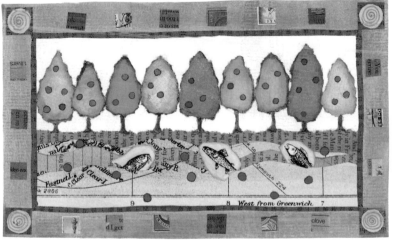

plain, while the wool from my flock can clothe them all." She took a piece of cooked meat from the cauldron, and it made the king's mouth water.

Now it was Cormac's turn to tell a truth. He told the couple about the fairy branch, and how it had cost him his wife and family. When he had finished, they brought out another piece of pork. The meat looked wonderful and Cormac was almost faint with hunger, but the memory of Ethne's abduction filled him with sorrow and he could not eat.

"What is the matter?" asked the man. "Is this meal not fit for a king?"

"Indeed it is," he replied, "but I am not accustomed to taking food with so small a company. Normally, I dine with fifty of my warriors."

The couple began to chant a lullaby which sent the king to sleep. On waking, fifty of his finest warriors were about him and Ethne, Carpre, and Ailbe were seated at the head of the table. Cormac rushed to them, vowing that his family should never again leave his sight.

Then the tall stranger identified himself. "Greetings, Cormac. I am Manannan mac Lir and this is my domain, the Land of Promise. It was I who visited you as a youth to give you my fairy branch, and I who raised the mist which brought you to this place. It pleases me now to see you reunited with your loved ones."

Cormac was keen to learn more about the marvels that he had witnessed, and Manannan was happy to enlighten him.

"The horsemen that you saw were foolish fortune-hunters, seeking wealth and cattle while the goods that they own wither and perish. The youth with the kindling wood labors in vain for the benefit of others, while never warming himself by his own fire. True wisdom is symbolized by the fountain. The five streams represent the five senses, the source of all human knowledge. No man shall be truly wise unless he drinks deeply from the fountain and each of its streams."

Cormac and his people ate and drank until a heavy sleep came upon them. When they awoke, they were by the walls of Tara, where they gave thanks for their homecoming. Cormac never again visited the Land of Promise, although he was reminded of it whenever he shook his fairy branch. It remained one of his most prized possessions, but as experience had taught him, the greatest treasure was his beloved Ethne.

THE LORDS OF IRUATH

As THE FAME AND REPUTATION of the Fianna grew, warriors flocked from every part of Ireland to join its ranks. Perhaps the strangest of these recruits were three brothers, the sons of the King of Iruath. They entered Fionn's court and offered their services, bringing with them a gigantic hound. This beast was larger than any dog the Fenians had ever seen, and all the colors of the world were visible on its coat.

The eldest of the brothers stepped forward to introduce himself. "I am Dubh the Dark," he declared. "I am skilled in the art of herbs and healing. If any of your companions are sick or wounded, bring them to me and I will cure their ills."

"My name is Agh the Battler," said the second man. "I will dispatch any foe who comes to ravage your domains. For no man alive can match the strength of my sword-arm or the power of my spear-throws."

Then the youngest of the trio spoke up. "I am known as Ilar the Eagle, my lord. With my keen eye, I will scout out the land for you, keeping watch for troublesome intruders. In addition, I can play the pipes so sweetly that my music will lull any man to sleep, no matter how hard he tries to stay awake."

"Our hound will also prove an asset," added Dubh, "for he has no peer as a tracker of game. Should your warrior-band ever fail to hunt down a deer or boar, he will always provide food for your table."

Fionn was delighted when he heard these words. "My friends, I bid you welcome. Come, sit with us now and join our fellowship." So saying, the leader of the Fianna beckoned the brothers forward. They held back, however, until Dubh came out with a curious request. "We thank you for your kind words, great lord, and look forward to serving you. Nevertheless, we must ask a boon of you. For reasons that we may not explain, we cannot lodge with your people. Instead, we must make our camp a little way off, surrounding it with a wall of fire. And, during the hours of darkness, none of your men may observe us or attempt to enter our circle of fire."

This was indeed a very strange demand, and it provoked a murmuring of discontent amongst some members of the Fianna. Fionn, however, waved away these objections, swayed by the thought of the great deeds that the lords of Iruath might perform in his service. Even so, he later spoke to the brothers in private, imploring them to reveal the reason for their unusual request. The princes looked at each other uncertainly until, after some hesitation, Dubh decided to speak. "The truth is, my liege, we are under an enchantment. Every night, one of us must die and the other two must watch over him. Provided that we keep this vigil, the stricken one will be restored to life as the sun rises. You will understand, I am sure, that we are anxious to ensure that nothing interferes with this crucial process. We beg you, therefore, to allow this matter to remain a secret."

Fionn was amazed at the brothers' story, scarcely knowing if he could believe it. Nevertheless, he agreed to respect their privacy and, from that time on, the lords of Iruath dwelt apart from the rest of the Fianna. This proved to be a wise decision, for the three princes soon had an opportunity to demonstrate the value of their service.

One bleak morning, three powerful strangers entered Fionn's court and demanded an audience with the leader of the Fianna. They were tall and strong, with flaming red hair, and by their sides there were

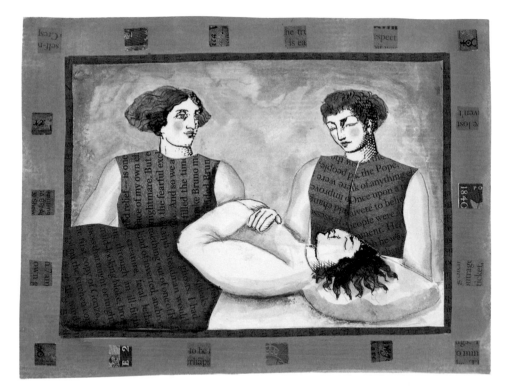

three vicious curs, each with snarling fangs and blood-red coats. "We are the sons of Uar," they announced, "and our names are Harm, Plunder, and Famine. A month ago, one of your warriors slew our father at the Battle of Bird-Mountain, and we have come to demand the blood-price for his death."

Immediately Fionn rose to his feet, incensed by the temerity of their request. "No one has ever paid me a blood-fine for any of my companions, who have been killed in battle, and by the same token I will never make any such payment for an enemy, who has been fairly slain in combat."

"Then we will take our own revenge," replied Harm, storming away with his brothers. Soon, the sons of Uar made good this threat. They built a fortified camp on Fionn's land and began to lay waste to the

surrounding countryside. There was scarcely a household which did not lose its cattle or its crops to the brothers; and scarcely a warrior who was not lamed or blinded by their swords.

Seeing the despair of the Fianna, Dubh approached Fionn and made him this promise. "My lord, we will rid you of the sons of Uar, if you follow these instructions. We will send our hound to make a circuit of your dwelling place. Three times it will course around your home, on three consecutive days. And on each occasion, there must be neither fire, nor weapons, nor any other dog within the building. Once these things have been performed, the sons of Uar will be defeated."

Fionn agreed to this willingly, knowing full well that the beast had magical qualities. The hound of Iruath was duly despatched and, while it was making its circuits of the building, Fionn's serving-maids noted how the air was filled with sweetness. It was as if a vat of mead was being strained, or a tub of fresh apples was being pulped.

After these rituals had been performed, the lords of Iruath led their hound into the camp of the enemy. There, the sons of Uar lay stricken with a strange weakness, caused by the enchantments of the three princes. Now the hound of Iruath opened its jaws and brought forth a venomous blast of air. Like a howling gale, its mighty breath lifted the villains out of their sickbeds, and hurled them out of their tents. Further and further they were thrown, until their bodies tumbled into the sea. A moment later, the sons of Uar vanished beneath the waves and were seen no more.

This victory inspired great rejoicing in the ranks of the Fianna. Fionn heaped praise upon the brothers and held a feast in their honor. Even so, there were some who viewed the celebrations with suspicion, believing that the trio were little more than sorcerers. The leaders of these doubters were two Munstermen, Donn and Dubhan. They led their followers up to the place where the lords of Iruath made their camp, determined to find out once and for all what lay behind the wall of fire.

So, in the dead of night, Donn and Dubhan put their cloaks over their heads and ran through the circle of flames. Inside, a strange sight greeted their eyes. Two of the brothers were seated on the ground, while the third lay stretched out, seemingly dead. On his chest sat the princes' hound, its jaws dripping with blood. The Munstermen were amazed at this spectacle and stopped in their tracks.

Then Dubh turned towards the intruders, saying bitterly, "So this is how Lord Fionn rewards our loyalty and service." With that, the hound leaped forward and opened its mouth. A ball of fire spouted forth, consuming the Munstermen and their followers. The flames burned the clothes from their backs and the flesh from their bones. Soon, there was nothing left but a heap of ashes.

Then, when dawn broke and their brother was restored to life, the lords of Iruath folded up their tents and slipped away. And they were never seen again by Fionn or any member of the Fianna.

THE CHASE OF SLIEVE GULLION

Dᴜʀɪɴɢ ʜɪꜱ ᴛɪᴍᴇ as the leader of the Fianna, Fionn mac Cumhaill was renowned for his flowing, golden locks. These were admired by many an Irish maid, among them Aine and Milucra, the fairy daughters of Culann the Smith. Both sisters were enamored of the warrior-hero and hoped to win his heart. One morning, as they walked together in the woods, Aine lavished praise upon his fine tresses, declaring that she could never love a man with hair of any other hue. This comment gave Milucra pause for thought, and she began to hatch a cunning plot.

Not long afterwards, Fionn went out hunting on the slopes of Slieve Gullion. His quarry was a pale fawn, which bounded up the hill with miraculous speed. Fionn had never witnessed a deer moving with such speed, but he was determined to catch it. Faster and faster it went as it sprang up the hill, before disappearing over a ridge. Fionn followed in hot pursuit but, as he climbed over the ridge, the creature was nowhere to be seen. Instead, he was greeted with the sight of a broad plateau and a tranquil lake.

By the edge of the water, a young woman sat, weeping piteously, and Fionn naturally went across to see what ailed her. As he drew nearer, he was struck by the force of her beauty. Her lips were as red as quicken berries, her neck was as white as apple blossom, and her eyes were as bright as the stars on a frosty night.

"What is it that causes you such distress, fair lady?" he enquired. "Tell me and I will do my best to help you, if it lies within my power."

The maid ceased her wailing and looked up at the stranger. "Sir," she replied, "I weep because I have lost my most prized possession, a ring of burnished gold which was given to me by my father. It has fallen into the water and I am unable to retrieve it. Could you find it for me?"

"Nothing simpler," declared Fionn and, casting off his coat, he dived into the lake. Three times he swam around it, searching in every crevice, until at last he lighted on the ring. Joyfully, he carried it out of the water and returned it to the maid. She grasped the bauble eagerly and gave a triumphant laugh. "Milucra thanks you for your assistance, noble lord", she exclaimed. Then, without further ado, she leaped into the lake and disappeared.

Fionn was bemused by her behavior, but his confusion was soon replaced by alarm. A strange weakness came over him and, looking down, he was horrified to find that his body had taken on the form of a wizened old man. His flesh was pale and wrinkled, and his golden hair had turned as white as snow. Only now did he begin to realize that he had been tricked into entering an enchanted pool, which had wrought a magical transformation upon him.

When the warriors of the Fianna saw what had happened to their stricken leader, they were filled with shock and anger. Immediately, they swore a solemn oath, vowing to take their revenge upon the sorceress. First, they built a wickerwork litter, raised on slender poles, which they used to carry their frail chief. Then they set off towards the fairy mound, where Milucra had her dwelling. There, they began to burrow away at the earth, determined to dig her out of her subterranean retreat. For three days and three nights, they labored tirelessly, before finally breaking through into the buried chamber.

Now Milucra emerged into the light and confronted the Fianna. In her right hand, she carried a golden drinking horn, which she held out towards them. "Forgive me, lords", she said, "for I never meant to harm your valiant leader. It was love, not hate, which made me act in this way. Take this vessel to Fionn and let him drink the potion. Once this is done, his youthful looks will be restored."

Milucra's wishes were obeyed and the horn was brought to the warrior-hero. Swiftly, he raised it to his lips and drank the draught. As he did so, the vessel gleamed and grew hot, and Fionn could no longer hold on to it. Falling to the ground, it was immediately swallowed up by the earth. Bubbles of steam frothed on the surface, but although

Fionn's companions wasted no time in searching for it, the horn had vanished completely.

Despite this, the potion had done its work. Fionn climbed down from his litter. His back straightened up and his skin became smooth once more. Only his hair still bore the marks of age, remaining a silvery white, just as the fairy had intended. Some members of the Fianna moved towards Milucra, as if to threaten her again, but Fionn restrained them with a motion of his hand. For in truth, he was content with the new color of his hair and chose to keep it that way. In this respect, Milucra's plan had succeeded, though it availed her nought. For Fionn never returned to hunt on the slopes of Slieve Gullion, and never again beheld the daughter of Culann.

THE BIRTH OF OISIN

It HAPPENED ONE TIME that Fionn and his followers went out
hunting in the dark woods around Almu. As they were returning home
empty-handed, a beautiful fawn sprang out of a covert and ran across
their path. Immediately, the whole company gave chase, anxious to
make up for the disappointments of the day. But the fawn was

extremely fleet of foot, and it soon began to outpace its pursuers. One by one, the huntsmen fell away, until only Fionn and his two hounds remained in the chase.

At length, the fawn ran out of the woods and entered a broad valley. There, it came to a halt and lay down on the grass. The hounds, Bran and Sceolan, quickly caught up with it but, to Fionn's surprise, they made no attempt to harm it. Instead, they scampered playfully around the creature, licking its face and neck. "This is no ordinary fawn," thought Fionn. So he set his weapons aside and turned to go home. As he did this, the fawn began to follow him. Indeed, it continued to follow him all the way back to Almu, with the hounds still playing by its feet. After they had arrived at his stronghold, Fionn gave orders that no one was to harm the creature and that it was to be allowed to roam freely around his home.

That same night, Fionn was roused from his slumbers, when a beautiful young woman walked into his chamber. Her dress was made of a rich, shimmering material, and she had the demeanour of a gracious queen. "Hail, noble Fionn!" she announced. "Thank you for giving shelter to a poor, hunted creature. My name is Sadb, and I am the fawn that you pursued today. Three years ago, Far Doirche, the Dark Druid, put me into that shape for spurning his advances. Since

then, I have lived a life of terror, ever fearing that I would meet my end at the jaws of a huntsman's dogs. Even today, I could not stop running until I had shaken off all but Bran and Sceolan, for I sensed that their nature was close to my own and that they would not harm me. Now, thanks to your kindness, I have returned to my former state, for the druid's spells have no power within the walls of your palace."

Fionn was amazed at the lady's tale of woe and invited her to remain with him. Soon, they fell in love and were married. Indeed, such was their passion that Fionn scarcely left his stronghold. He gave up hunting and other outdoor pursuits, preferring to remain at Almu with Sadb.

This happy state of affairs finally came to an end, when raiders from Lochlann landed on Erin's shores and embarked on a campaign of looting and pillaging. Much against his will, Fionn bowed to his duty and made ready for battle. Before leaving, however, he bade his wife a fond farewell, promising to return as soon as possible. His sorrow at this parting was all the more painful, because Sadb was now bearing his child.

Fionn was as good as his word. He launched a ferocious attack upon the foreigners, driving them back into the sea. So, within the space of just seven days, he was able to lead his army home in triumph. He sent

messengers ahead with the news and, as the familiar towers of Almu
came into view, he hoped that he might see some acknowledgement of
the victory – a banner of welcome, perhaps, or his wife watching from
the ramparts.

Instead, an air of despondency hung over the palace. His people
seemed subdued, and no one dared to look him in the eye. Worse still,
there was no sign of his beloved. "Where is Sadb?" he cried out. "Where
is the flower of Almu? Why is she not here to greet me?" There was a
heavy silence, before one of his men plucked up the courage to reply.

"While you were away, my lord, your wife walked on the ramparts all
day long, eagerly watching out for your return. At length, two days ago,
she saw you walking on the fields below with Bran and Sceolan..."

"Two days ago, I was still fighting the enemy," Fionn snapped.

"I know, my lord, but this man was the very image of you. Besides,
we thought we heard the hunting call of the Fianna echoing in the
distance. In any event, Sadb wasted no time in rushing down to greet
you. Before we could stop her, she had run out of the stronghold
towards the man with the two dogs. The moment she reached him,
however, she let out a piercing scream. For the stranger brought out a
druid wand from beneath his cloak, and tapped her on the shoulder
with it. Immediately, Sadb vanished from our sight, transformed once

more into a docile fawn. Three times, she tried to escape and make her way back to the palace but, on each occasion, the druid's hounds caught her by the throat and dragged her away. When we realized what was happening, we took up our arms and hurried out to help your lady. But, by the time we arrived, they had all disappeared: the sorcerer, the dogs and Sadb."

When he heard this sorry tale, Fionn beat his breast and moaned loudly. For he knew straight away that this dissembler must have been Far Doirche, the Dark Druid, who had come to reclaim his prize. Without further ado, he climbed back on his horse and called for his hounds, anxious to try and track them down. Then he rode out into the countryside around Almu, scouring every hill, every glen, and every forest. And the only hounds that he would have by his side were Bran and Sceolan, for he knew that they would never harm the fawn.

The chase proved fruitless, and Fionn returned home that night, sad and discouraged. But next morning, he rose early and continued his search, once again without success. Time passed. The days turned into weeks, the weeks turned into months; still, there was no sign of Sadb. Eventually, Fionn gave up, resigned to the fact that she was lost forever. Gradually, he began to resume his former pursuits, feasting at Almu with his companions and hunting with the Fianna.

73

It was during one of these hunts that a curious thing occurred. On the slopes of Ben Bulben, his hounds caught the scent of an unusual prey. They chased it through thickets and brambles, before eventually trapping it in a narrow place. Then they barked, loudly and urgently, until Fionn and his men arrived. The sight of this quarry astonished the Fianna, for it was a naked young boy, covered entirely in hair. Stranger still, Bran and Sceolan started to lick the child affectionately, just as they had licked the fawn.

Fionn looked closely at the lad and fancied that he saw some likeness of Sadb. Could this be the child that she was carrying, when Far Doirche had abducted her? Fionn was unsure but, even so, he gave orders that the boy should be taken back to Almu and raised in his household.

Little by little, the child lost his wildness and began to learn the use of speech. In time, this enabled him to tell Fionn about his early days. He had known neither father nor mother, he said, save for a tender fawn, which fed him and sheltered him. They had lived together happily in a secluded valley, but their life had been blighted by a dark, shadowy man, who had visited them there. Many a time he would talk with the fawn, sometimes addressing it with cajoling words, but more often with anger or threats.

At last, there came a time when the stranger's patience was exhausted. He drew out a hazel rod and struck both of them with it. This blow seemed to cast an enchantment on them, for the fawn was compelled to follow the man, even though she struggled hard to resist. As for himself, he had tried to follow, but his legs were rooted to the spot. He fought hard against this spell, but it was useless. In the end, all he could do was listen helplessly to the piteous cries of the fawn, as they grew fainter and fainter. When he could no longer hear her at all, his senses began to swim and he fell to the ground. When he awoke, he was alone on the side of a hill, near the spot where Bran and Sceolan had found him. And, though he searched far and wide, he could never find the valley again.

Then Fionn knew that he had found his son. He gave him the name Oisin, which means "little fawn", and raised him as his heir. In due course, Oisin grew up to be a fine poet, a valiant warrior, and a worthy member of the Fianna. Fionn was justly proud of him, though his pride was tinged with sadness. In his heart, he still hoped that he might find Sadb one day, but their paths never crossed again.

THE DEATH OF DIARMAID

Diarmaid remained one of the mightiest members of the
Fianna, but in later years there was bitter enmity between him and
Fionn. The source of this hostility was Diarmaid's elopement with
Gráinne, Fionn's betrothed. Then, after many years of strife,
their feud was eventually resolved by Oenghus, the god of love.
In time, Fionn went on to marry a different bride, while Diarmaid
and Gráinne lived happily together and raised four sons. It
seemed that the two men had forgotten their differences,
but Fionn's resentment still lingered, awaiting a suitable moment
for revenge.

Now it happened one summer that Fionn and his companions were
invited to stay at Diarmaid's stronghold. For many a day, there was
laughter and feasting in his hall. But, on the final night of the visit,
Diarmaid was roused from his sleep by the sound of a barking dog. He
wanted to go out and investigate, but Gráinne called him back,
convinced that the noise was due to some mischief of the fairy folk.
Reluctantly, Diarmaid consented and climbed back into bed. A few
moments later, the barking started up a second time and Gráinne had
to quell his curiosity once more. On the third occasion, however, there
was no holding him back. Diarmaid rose up and donned his hunting
gear, before setting off in search of the hound.

He rode until morning, following the noise of the dog. At length, he found himself on the heights of Ben Bulben, where Fionn and the Fianna were engaged in a boar hunt. There, Fionn informed him that they were on the scent of a magical boar, which had neither ears nor tail. Its strength was unsurpassed, however, and it had already slain no fewer than thirty men, that very morning. "My companions are chasing it this way now, so that I may do battle with it," Fionn continued. "It would be better for you, however, if you took cover." The chief of the Fianna uttered these words, knowing full well that his enemy's pride and honor would never allow him to take such a cowardly course.

"I have no fear of any wild beast," Diarmaid declared. "I will stand here with you and fight by your side."

"That would be most unwise," said Fionn, "for there is a taboo against you hunting any kind of boar."

Diarmaid was surprised by this news. "I have never heard of any such restriction," he replied.

"I remember it well," Fionn explained, "though it happened when you were but a child. Your father, Donn, sent you to be raised in the household of Oenghus, where you were fostered together with the son of a steward. Both of you were fine children, but the steward's son had a charm and grace, which endeared him greatly to the serving people in

Oenghus's house. This favoritism stirred Donn's resentment. In a fit of rage, he cracked the boy's skull and threw him to the dogs. As you can imagine, the steward was distraught and demanded justice. Your father refused this, believing that the man was nothing more than an underling. However, the steward was well versed in the dark arts, so he took his druid wand and transformed his dead son into a wild boar; one that had neither ears nor a tail. Then he placed a curse on you, son of Donn, vowing that this boar would be the cause of thy death. So, from that moment on, Oenghus placed a strict taboo upon you, forbidding you to hunt any sort of boar. In this way, he hoped that you might be spared from the steward's vengeance."

Fionn smiled as he recited this story, but Diarmaid's spirits sank. He had long since forgotten the stricture, which had been placed on him in his youth, and felt sure that his rival had organized this boar hunt expressly, to bring about his doom. Despite this, his honor as a knight of the Fianna was at stake, so he stood his ground and awaited the arrival of the boar.

The beast was not slow in coming. In a moment, it appeared over the brow of the hill and raced towards Diarmaid. With a heavy heart, he noticed that it had no ears and was, without a doubt, the steward's son. Nevertheless, he swiftly loosed his hound, hoping that it might

distract the boar. But the dog shied away, fearing for its life. Then Diarmaid raised his trusty spear and hurled it at the enchanted boar. The weapon struck the beast on its snout, but it did not even scratch its skin and fell uselessly to the ground. Next, Diarmaid drew his sword and smote the boar's neck with all his power, but the blade shattered into a thousand pieces, leaving the hero defenseless.

Now the boar rushed again, inflicting a deep and ghastly wound in the warrior's side. But, as the beast came in for the kill, Diarmaid wrestled it to the ground and rammed the hilt of his sword against the boar's skull. It penetrated the creature's brain, killing it stone dead.

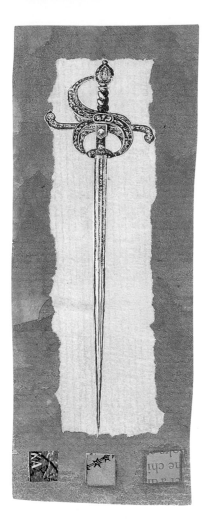

As Diarmaid lay in agony on the earth, the chief of the Fianna came
over to him, followed closely by his men. "It pleases me greatly to see
you in this state," said Fionn. "I only wish that all the women in
Ireland could see you at this moment. For, in spite of your love-spot,
your beauty has fled. The face that was once so handsome is now pale
and deformed."

Diarmaid ignored these harsh words and began to plead for his life.
"Heal me, my lord, as you know you can," he gasped. For it was

common knowledge that Fionn had the power to restore health and
vigor to any man, if he brought him a drink of water cupped in
his hands.

"Why should I?" said Fionn. "Surely, of all the men in this world,
you are the least deserving of my mercy."

Then Diarmaid reminded him of the many services which he had
rendered to him, in expiation of his guilt. He also recalled the mighty
exploits that he had performed over the years for the greater glory of
the Fianna. These words brought a murmur of approval from the
assembled company, and Fionn's companions urged him to save the
dying hero.

Reluctantly, the vengeful chieftain walked across to a nearby spring
and cupped some water in his hands. But, as he turned back towards
Diarmaid, he deliberately let the water slip through his fingers. His
warriors noticed this and urged him angrily to try again. So Fionn
went to the spring for a second time and gathered some water. But, as
he moved towards Diarmaid, he thought of Gráinne, his lost bride, and
his fury caused him to let the water spill to the ground. As he did so,
Diarmaid gave a loud sigh of anguish.

Then Oscar stepped forward from the ranks of the Fianna and
railed at his leader. "I swear to you, my lord, that if you do not bring

82

water without further delay, then either you or I will die on this hill today." His words were echoed by other members of the company, so Fionn finally relented and fetched the water in his cupped hands. This action came too late, however, for by the time that he sprinkled the liquid on Diarmaid's lips, the warrior had already breathed his last.

When they saw this, the Fianna uttered a great wail of lamentation, which reverberated across the plains of Erin. So loud was this cry of despair that it reached the ears of Oenghus, who was in his fairy mound at Brug na Búinne. He came with his people and raised the body of Diarmaid onto a golden litter, which they carried back with great ceremony to the love god's dwelling. There, Oenghus gave vent to his grief for the loss of his noble foster-son. As for the Fianna, they did not forget the treacherous actions of their chief, and Fionn's leadership of the company soon drew to a close.

The Children of Lir

AFTER THEIR DEFEAT at the Battle of Tailltin, the Danaan lords of
Ireland assembled to choose a king for themselves. For, they reasoned,
they would be less likely to suffer a similar humiliation in the future, if
they were united under the leadership of a strong leader.

Now the chief candidates for this honor were Bodb and Oenghus,
two of the Dagda's sons, Midir the Proud, and Lir of Sid Finnachaid.
The arguments went on long and hard, before eventually Bodb was
selected. Everyone accepted this choice apart from Lir. In a fit of
jealousy, he stormed away from the assembly, refusing to acknowledge
the new king. This caused great anger among the Danaans, and some
lords were determined to make war on Lir and burn his palace to the
ground. Bodb restrained them, however, anxious that his reign should
be marked by peace, rather than strife.

Nevertheless, resentment simmered among many of the Danaans,
until a cruel stroke of fate offered a chance for reconciliation. Lir's
wife died, and the rebel lord was consumed with grief. Now Bodb
displayed his regal qualities. Magnanimously, he sent word to Lir,
consoling him for his loss and offering him the hand of one of his
three beloved foster-daughters. There was no doubting the generosity
of this gesture, for everyone knew that these three maids were Bodb's
greatest treasures.

Lir was overwhelmed by the king's kindness. Joy and remorse mingled in his heart, as he traveled to Bodb's palace to accept the offer. There, he was married with Aobh, the oldest of the three foster-children. For fourteen days, the couple remained with Bodb and his people, feasting and rejoicing. After this, they returned to Lir's home at Sid Finnachaid, where the celebrations continued.

The match proved a blissful one and, in the course of time, Aobh gave birth to two sets of twins. The oldest pair was a daughter named Finola and a boy named Aedh, while the younger ones were two sons, Conn and Fiachra. But misfortune still lingered over the house of Lir, for Aobh died in childbirth, casting the unhappy man into a mood of deep despondency. Indeed, but for the comfort of his four little children, he might well have succumbed to his grief.

When Bodb came to hear of this new tragedy, he shared Lir's sense of loss. He mourned for the memory of his favorite foster-child but, at the same time, he was also determined that the bonds between the two families should not be broken. With this in mind, he offered Lir the hand of Aoife, his second foster-daughter.

Lir was grateful for this act of generosity and, once again, he made the journey to Bodb's palace. There, the marriage was celebrated with great pomp and dignity. Both men were pleased to renew their friendship but, in view of Aobh's recent death, the festivities were inevitably more muted than before.

At the end of fourteen days, the couple traveled back to Sid Finnachaid, where Aoife was introduced to her new stepchildren. For a time, all went well. Lir gradually recovered from Aobh's death, taking every opportunity to comfort himself by playing with his precious infants. For her part, Aoife seemed equally fond of them. She nursed them tenderly, showering them with the same love and affection that her sister would have shown. More than this, she would often take them to her father's palace, so that he too could fuss over them. Indeed, Bodb would give them the place of honor at his table, so that everyone could see that these were the fairest children in Ireland.

As the months passed by, however, Aoife began to resent these attentions. Did her husband not neglect her, in favor of these babes? Did her father not display more affection to them, than he ever had to her, his own foster-daughter? Gradually, these things started to rankle with her, and her love for Aobh's children turned to hate. Then, as jealousy gnawed away at her heart, she began to plan her revenge.

Not long after this, Aoife took to her bed, feigning illness. For the best part of a year, she remained there brooding and plotting, until Lir despaired of her ever being well again. Then one day, she rose suddenly from her bed and gave orders for horses to be yoked to her chariot. After this, she announced to her husband that she was taking the children on a visit to Bodb's palace. Lir agreed to this willingly, so delighted was he by his wife's unexpected recovery.

When Aoife sent her serving women to make ready the children, however, a problem arose. In the night, Finola had suffered a terrible dream, which convinced her that she and her brothers were in mortal danger. Because of this, she refused to leave home, and urged her siblings to stay with her. But Aoife's hatred burned fiercely within her, and she would not be deflected from her purpose. Accordingly, she took the child to Lir, asking him to calm her. With the gentlest of paternal cares, he soothed Finola, assuring her that her fears were

nothing more than phantoms of the night, and eventually she
agreed to go.

So Aoife set off with her stepchildren. All went well, until they
reached a lonely place at the edge of Lake Darvra, where she ordered
the chariot to stop. There she took her minions to one side and bade
them kill the younglings. "Dispatch them now," she commanded, "and I
will give you more riches than you can imagine. For these accursed
children have cost me the love of my husband, and I can never regain
it until they are gone."

These words filled her attendants with horror. Swiftly, they shrank
away from her and refused to carry out the evil deed. Disgusted by their
weakness, Aoife laid hands on a sword and resolved to kill them
herself. But her courage failed her, so instead she led the children
down to the edge of the lake and instructed them to bathe in its waters.
They did her bidding, little knowing the danger they were in. For, as
soon as they were in the lake, Aoife pulled out a druid wand and struck
the water. As she did so, a terrible transformation came over the
children. They moaned in anguish, as their spirits were torn from their
bodies and changed into the guise of four, snow-white swans.

Aoife, meanwhile, gloated at the success of her plan. "Away with
you, cursed creatures," she called out. "Make what you can of your new

home on this lake, for you will never again set eyes on your
native land."

The children of Lir listened to these words with dismay; for, despite
their transformation, they were still able to speak and understand the
human tongue. Finola led their complaints, saying: "Evil woman, why
have you done this to us? What mischiefs did we commit, which caused
your friendship to change to treachery? Do not think that your foul
deed will go unpunished for, if there is any justice in this world, the
doom that awaits you shall be far worse than ours."

But Aoife was unrepentant. "Away with you and your threats. You
will never have the means to avenge yourselves on me. For nine

hundred years, you will remain in your feathered state; three hundred here at Lake Darvra, another three hundred on the stormy Sea of Moyle, and yet three hundred more in the chilly climes of Irros Domnann, on the Western Sea. Only when you hear the sound of a Christian bell will you know that release is at hand. Until then, I will grant you only one boon. You may keep your human voices, and I will make them as sweet as the voices of the fairy people, so that anyone who hears them may be lulled into a gentle sleep. That is the extent of my mercy. Now begone, I have finished with you!"

With these words, Aoife turned her back on the lake and mounted her chariot. Within moments, she had gone, thundering away towards the palace of her foster-father. There, as usual, she was greeted with great warmth and affection. This reception became chillier, however, when she explained the reason for the absence of the children.

"Lir no longer loves you," said Aoife. "Indeed, he has become so mistrustful that he believes his children would be in danger if he allowed them to accompany me here."

Bodb was baffled by this news. "What has brought about this sudden change?" he wondered. "Surely he must know that I dote upon his children and would never let them come to any harm." Aoife had no answer to this, but merely shrugged, and this aroused the king's

suspicions. So, when she was ensconced in her chamber, he secretly
sent messengers to Lir, enquiring after the welfare of the children.

The arrival of these envoys alarmed Lir greatly. Immediately, he
called for his chariot and made ready to depart to see what had
become of his babes. His route took him past Lake Darvra where he
noticed four beautiful swans swimming towards him. He marveled at
the sweetness of their song, and wondered even more when he realized
that their voices were human. "Father," cried the largest of the swans,
"what sorrow awaits you here! We are your offspring, transformed into
swans through the evil spells of our stepmother."

When Lir heard these dreadful tidings, he fell to his knees and wept.
"Is there any way that this wickedness may be undone?" he sobbed.

"None at all," replied Finola. "Nor may we follow you home, for
Aoife has imprisoned us on this lake, and we are bound to remain here
for the next three hundred years."

Lir wept still more, as this awful truth sank in. Then he told his
people to make camp, for he had decided to spend the night by the side
of the lake. There, his children sang for him, and their sweet fairy
music eased his sorrow and lulled him into a tranquil sleep.

Next morning, Lir rose with the dawn, eager to take revenge on his
villainous wife. So, after bidding a fond farewell to his children, he

hastened onward to Bodb's palace. There, he informed the king of the terrible fate of his children, imploring him to bring Aoife to justice. Bodb needed no second bidding. In a voice that trembled with fury, he commanded that his foster-daughter should be brought before him.

When Aoife appeared, Bodb rebuked her sternly for her dreadful deed and bemoaned the evil day when he first accepted her into his household. Then he gave her into the care of his druids, bidding them to turn her into the foulest and meanest of all creatures. They readily obeyed and, striking her with their wands, they changed Aoife into a demon of the air. Racked with pain and anguish, she was doomed to drift helplessly amid the clouds until the end of time.

Then Bodb and all the Danaan lords returned with Lir to the shores of Darvra. There, they marveled at the beauty of the swans and listened with rapture to their balming melodies, wafting across the placid waters of the lake. This was the first of many such visits, for although Aoife's spell could not be undone, every single one of Bodb's subjects was determined to comfort the children as far as possible.

In this way, the first part of Aoife's curse was endured with comparatively little hardship. But, after three hundred years, the swans were forced to fly off to the lonely Sea of Moyle. There, they were

starved of all human company, and their gentle lullabies turned into
plaintive laments. For three long centuries they languished there,
drenched by waves, buffeted by storms and tossed by tempests. If this
seemed bad, then the chilly wastes of Irrus Domnann were even worse.
There, the sea turned to ice and the swans became frozen onto rocks,
unable to escape until the season changed. During these dark days,
Finola tried to comfort her brothers, urging them to place their trust in
God, for He would deliver them from their misery.

At long last, the cruel sentence passed by Aoife drew to a close.
After thrice three hundred years, the swans of Lir were free to leave the
Western Sea and travel where they wished. With one accord, their first
resolve was to return to their old home at Sid Finnachaid. The journey
was long and arduous, but there was gladness in their hearts,

particularly when they flew over some hill or forest that they
remembered from their youth.

Eventually, the familiar haunts of their childhood came into view
and the swans prepared to alight. As they did so, a terrible sight met
their eyes. Sid Finnachaid had undergone a transformation as
terrible as their own. Its ramparts were broken, its walls were
covered with moss, and their father's palace lay desolate and empty.
Weeds and brambles covered everything that remained of their
former lives.

Now Finola gave voice to the sorrow which they shared: "O
brothers, what has become of this place? Where is our father, whom we
ached to see? Where are the carefree youths who used to play with us?
Where are the conquering heroes with their glittering swords, the
huntsmen with their eager hounds, the revelers with their brimming
goblets? Is everyone that we knew now stilled and dead? Is nothing left
of Sid Finnachaid's glories but this rank decay?"

With heavy hearts, the swans spent that night amid the ruins of their
childhood home, bitterly recalling the happy days of long ago and
heaping new curses on the memory of Aoife. Next day, however, they
flew off, for it gave them no pleasure to linger in the wreckage of the
past. At length, they made a new home on Inis Glora, an island in the

Western Sea. Here they dwelt contentedly for many years, filling the air with the sweetness of their songs.

During these years, the land of Erin entered a new age. St. Patrick came and spread the word of God across the land. Others followed in his wake, holy men who built chapels and churches on the ruins of the fairy mounds. Such a man was St. Kennock, a hermit who settled on Inis Glora. One morning, the swans heard the bell from his oratory echoing across the waters. The brothers took fright at this, for the sound was new and strange to them, but Finola was joyful. "Do you not see, my friends, this is the voice of the Christian bell, and it signals that our suffering is nearing its end."

At once, the swans rose up, following the ringing of the bell, until it led them to St. Kennock. Then they began to sing, and their chanting delighted the holy man, for it seemed more heavenly to him than any

sound he had ever heard. "Are you the fabled birds of Lir?" he asked.

"Most certainly, we are," they chorused.

Then Kennock rejoiced, explaining that he had chosen to settle on Inis Glora on their account, preferring it to all other islands. Their story was well known, he added, and he hoped that, with the help of God, he could bring an end to their sufferings.

As he spoke these words, a miraculous transformation ensued. The feathers and the bird-skins fell away, and the offspring of Lir were returned to human form. They were children no longer, however, but wizened ancients, with hair and skin as white as their plumage had been. "Come, holy man," cried Finola, "baptize us quickly, for our days are at an end. Shed no tears for us, for it is a source of great relief that we have cast off our bird-like shapes at last."

The holy man obeyed. Then, when the four had breathed their last, he buried them in a single grave. Above it, he set a pillar-stone, marked with an ogham inscription. Then, as he recited his final blessing, he fancied that he saw a radiant vision of four innocent children, each with silvery wings and blissful expressions. They seemed to smile down at him for an instant, before spreading their wings and swooping upward, to find their place in heaven.

THE EXPLOITS OF CÚ CHULAINN

OF ALL THE HEROES in Ireland, none was more powerful or more courageous than Cú Chulainn, the champion of Ulster. Blessed with superhuman strength from the day of his birth, he became the supreme master of combat. In his youth, he traveled to the Isle of Shadows, where a warrior-queen named Scáthach trained him in the arts of war. From her, he learned how to juggle nine apples in the air and hurl them at approaching foes; from her, he acquired the skill of balancing on the point of a spear and catching a javelin in full flight; from her, he developed the hero's scream, which could cause an enemy to drop

dead with fright. More than all of these, it was Scáthach who gave him his most potent weapon, the *gae bolga*, a fearsome spear which could rip out a man's innards.

These talents were put to the test when Maeve, the warrior-queen of Connacht, brought her army into Ulster in order to steal a magic bull. At this time the men of Ulster lay under a curse which left them powerless to fight. Cú Chulainn alone was immune from this spell, and so the struggle fell squarely on his shoulders. By night, he harried the enemy from a distance, splitting many a skull with the stones from his sling; by day he defeated the cream of the Connacht army in single combat.

With mounting desperation, Maeve sent champion after champion to confront the Ulsterman, but all were vanquished. Indeed, his fiercest battles were not with mortal foes, but with the Morrigan, the shape-shifting goddess of war. One morning, for example, when he was duelling in the river with Loch mac Emonis, he felt a sharp tugging at his heel. It was a huge, black eel, which wound itself around his feet and sent him tumbling into the drink. As he lay there, Loch flailed at him with his sword, reddening the water with the Ulsterman's blood.

Rising up, Cú Chulainn grabbed hold of the eel and dashed it against a stone, breaking its back. Instinctively, the creature loosened its grip but, in an instant, it had changed into a snarling she-wolf. With

a bound, it leaped out onto the bank and sent a herd of cattle stampeding against the stricken hero. Undaunted, Cú Chulainn readied his sling and sent a sharp stone speeding into the wolf's left eye. It recoiled, howling in pain, while at that same moment, Loch's sword cut into the Ulsterman's thigh.

Now the Morrigan assumed her final form, a hornless red heifer that hurtled toward him. Once again, Cú Chulainn loosed a stone from his sling, which broke the animal's legs. The heifer sank to the ground with a sigh and came at him no more. Turning his attention to his human foe, Cú Chulainn brought out the *gae bolga* and sent it skimming along the surface of the water. As it always did, the weapon found its mark and Loch fell dead at his feet.

Wearily, Cú Chulainn climbed out of the river and looked for a suitable place to tend his wounds. As he walked, he came across a crippled, one-eyed hag milking a cow. It was a sorry-looking beast, for it only had three teats, but the sight of it filled the warrior with a burning thirst. So he asked the crone for a drink of milk, and she readily obliged.

The milk tasted better than anything Cú Chulainn had ever drunk before, so he thanked the hag effusively. "May your generosity bring you good health," he declared. And, as he spoke these words, the woman's back straightened up a little. Immediately, she handed him a drink from the second teat. It tasted even better than the first, and Cú Chulainn swallowed it greedily. Then he repeated his blessing on the crone, wishing her the best of health. As he did so, the woman stretched her leg and it was clear that she was no longer lame.

Without being asked, the hag then gave the Ulsterman a drink from the final teat. This was the best yet, and he blessed her once again for the gift. Now the woman turned to look at him, and it was plain that her missing eye had been restored. On her face, there was a sinister smile that Cú Chulainn knew all too well.

"Thank *you*, my lord, for your blessings have made me whole again," said the Morrigan.

"If I had known it was you," said Cú Chulainn bitterly, "I would never have opened my mouth."

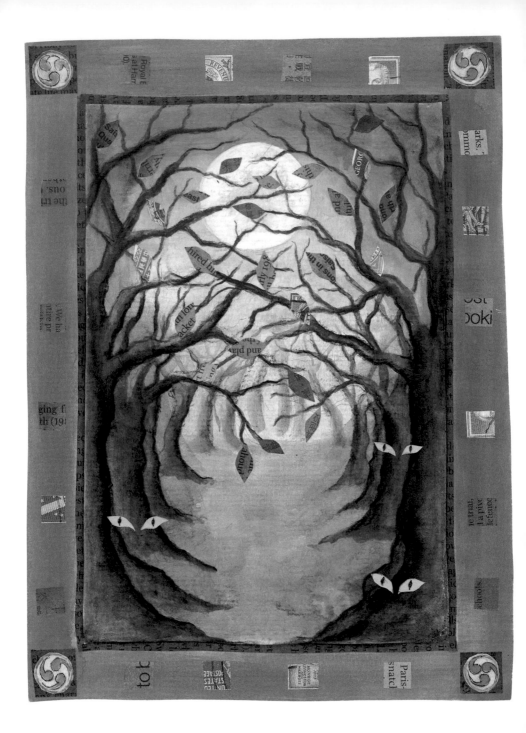

LEGENDS
OF THE POOKA

PEGGY OF THE CROOKED BACK

Everybody in the village knew Peggy Barrett. In her youth, she had been a noted beauty and the finest dancer in the district. Now however, as she entered her eightieth year, she was better known for the cruel deformity, which had earned her the nickname of "Peggy of the Crooked Back". For as long as anyone could remember, she had been afflicted with a hideous, misshapen back, which made it impossible for her to stand upright.

Away from her presence, the local children would make fun of her, calling her "the hunchback" or "the walking table". No one dared to do this to her face. For, even with her deformity, Peggy had a commanding air, never more so than when she was regaling the children with her fables and stories. These were full of menacing goblins and wicked fairies, and the youngsters always listened with rapt attention. One tale, above all, impressed them. This was the story which she repeated every year, at the end of April; the only one, she insisted, which was true in every respect.

The arrival of Spring was a happy time in the village. Young girls busied themselves making goaling-balls for the hurling match and cutting up ribbons for the mummers who would perform at the May Day festivities. But, as Peggy reminded the children, the celebrations were also a reminder of darker and more sinister times. For May Eve

coincided with the old feast of Beltane, the witches' day, when spirits of
every kind roamed abroad. It was a day, Peggy stressed, when every
child would be well advised to make sure that they were indoors before
evening came.

"I had heard tales of horror from my elders," she recalled, "but I was
young and foolish and thought nothing of such things. What were a
few imps and fairies to me? How could they possibly cause me any
harm? These were my sentiments on one particular May Eve, many
years ago, when I failed to return home on time. The day had been
bright and sunny, fresh blossoms hung on the trees, and the world
seemed so full of sweetness and innocence that I lost all track of time.

None of the old stories bothered me until a thin mist began to rise as I walked back across the fields. Suddenly, it occurred to me that I would not reach home before dark and a sense of foreboding stirred within me.

I quickened my step, but the light and warmth of the day ebbed swiftly away. By the time I arrived at the crossroads, the sun had already set. It was darker still on the forest path, where the tall trees arched above me, blocking out the light of the moon. Then, as I hurried on, I fancied that I heard a rustling amid the branches. I told myself that it must be my imagination but, as I glanced to my right, I saw something resembling a black goat with long, curving horns. It was standing on its hind legs, its forelegs resting against a bough, and it seemed to be staring directly at me.

I broke into a run, telling myself that the edge of the village lay close at hand. I had only gone a few paces further, however, when I heard another rustling sound. This time, the noise came from my left.

Hardly daring to look, I turned my head, only to be confronted with a more terrible sight. The same goat-like creature was watching me. Now, however, it had grown to three times its original size, and was taller than the tallest man.

Blind panic took hold of me, and I ran as I had never run before. But, however fast I managed to move, the ominous sounds from the undergrowth made it clear that the beast was keeping pace with me. Suddenly, I heard a whistling noise from above and then a heavy thud, as something landed on my back. It was the creature. Its forelegs clamped themselves on my shoulders, while the hind ones locked around my waist.

How I stopped myself from falling I shall never know, but I somehow managed to keep going. The weight of the beast slowed me down and its hot breath burned the back of my neck, but I was determined to reach safety. Already, I could see a house in the distance. I called out, but nobody seemed to hear me. Then, as I drew nearer, I could hear the sounds of laughter and merrymaking from within. I called out again and banged hard on the door, but the place was barred and shuttered. The inhabitants knew better than to leave a window open at Beltane.

I came to a halt and rested my hands against my knees. The burden on my back seemed heavier than ever. Then, in my despair, I cried out for help to St. Brigit and blessed myself. Nothing happened. I invoked the saint's name a second time, begging for her mercy. Still nothing. The weight now became even heavier and I gave myself up for lost. A third time I called out, imploring heaven to take pity on my soul. This time, as the words left my lips, I heard a mighty crack, as deafening as a clap of thunder. The door in front of me flew open and the beast sprang away from my shoulders. I fell to my knees and tears welled up in my eyes; tears of pain and tears of gratitude."

As Peggy neared the end of her story, she gazed down at her young audience, seated on the floor. "And that, my children, is how I come to be as you see me now. For, although my life was spared, I have never been able to straighten my back from that day to this."

The children looked up at Peggy in silence. It pleased her to note that, every time she told this tale, the youngsters would see her crooked back in a different light. It was no longer funny or ugly, but a powerful reminder of a terrifying encounter. And there was always one tiny voice, which would pipe up and ask the obvious question: "What was it that sat on your back?"

Then Peggy would answer with a grim smile, "It was the pooka, little one, and I pray that it never comes to sit on yours."

THE SPIRIT HORSE

THE GREEN FIELDS OF ERIN were not only home to gods and
warrior-heroes, but also to a whole panoply of demons and spirits. The
most feared of these was the pooka, a shape-shifting fairy who preyed
on unwary travellers.

Certainly, Murtagh Sullivan gave little thought to the pooka as he
embarked on a pilgrimage to the shrine of St. Gobnait. The journey
took him through a remote, mountainous district, criss-crossed with
unmarked pathways and tracks. Before long, he had taken a wrong
turning and become hopelessly lost. The afternoon wore on and, as
darkness approached, a thick fog began to descend. The unfortunate
pilgrim felt a surge of panic and prayed aloud for someone who would
rescue him from his predicament.

As the words left his lips, Murtagh spied a light in the distance, faint
and twinkling. Immediately, he headed toward it, hoping that it might
be some form of refuge where he could pass the night. Curiously,
though, the light seemed to come no nearer, even though Murtagh was
walking as fast as he could. "Perhaps it is a holy light," he mused, "sent
by St. Gobnait herself to guide me out of this terrible place."

With this in mind, Murtagh offered up a further prayer. "If you have
sent this light for me, O wondrous one, then please allow me to see
your face, that I may worship you with all my heart." These words

seemed to have some effect because, as the minutes went by, the light appeared to grow larger. Gradually, it became clear that its source was an open fire, beside which an old woman was warming herself. Murtagh was surprised by this, since the shriveled creature bore no resemblance to the noble images of the saint which he had seen in church. Nor could he understand how the light of the fire had recently seemed to move. These doubts, however, were dwarfed by a sheer sense of relief at finding a fellow human being in this bleak terrain.

Murtagh walked boldly up to the fire, preparing to greet the woman. But as he opened his mouth, the old hag turned toward him and the sight of her face froze the pilgrim in his tracks. For the woman's eyes were not brown or blue or grey, but a deep, glowing red. Worse still, a sulphurous steam came from her lips when she spoke. "Who are you?" she demanded.

"Murtagh Sullivan, at your service," he stammered. "I am a humble pilgrim, on his way to visit the shrine of St. Gobnait." Murtagh wanted to fall to his knees at this very moment and call out for the saint's assistance, but he was rigid with fear. His body was no longer capable of making the slightest movement.

"You have lost your way," cackled the woman, "and there is no saint here to help you. Nevertheless, take hold of my hand and I'll lend you a horse, which will carry you to your journey's end." So saying, she rose from her place by the fire and grasped Murtagh's hand firmly. He wanted to pull away, but there was an unnatural strength in her grip and he was powerless to resist.

Then the crone led Murtagh along a steep track, rising up into the mountains. Soon, they arrived at a large cavern, hollowed out of the rock. As they drew near, Murtagh could hear the clanging of giant hooves and a fearsome whinnying. Suddenly, an enormous black horse emerged from the chamber, stamping its feet impatiently. Murtagh recoiled in front of the beast, but the woman pushed him forward. "Mount up, traveler. Climb onto his back and he will give you the ride of your life." Then, with a feat of strength which belied her hag-like form, she lifted Murtagh onto the horse's back.

Immediately, the animal took off, leaping from the mountain path into the chill, black void. With a desperate lunge, Murtagh managed to catch hold of its mane and held on grimly as it began to soar upward. Faster and faster it moved, hurtling past crags and crevices. Then, as it

reached the summit, the beast changed direction. Now it began to descend, plummeting toward a deep ravine. Murtagh could feel himself losing his balance, so he tried to tighten his grip on the mane. This time, however, his hands were left grasping at shadows, as the spirit horse dispersed, its limbs drifting apart like the wisps of a cloud. Now Murtagh was alone, falling swiftly into the darkness.

Next morning, a group of pilgrims found Murtagh Sullivan lying at the foot of the mountain. They gave him a Christian burial before continuing on their way, with each man offering up a silent prayer to St. Gobnait, to thank her for sparing him from the clutches of the pooka.

LEGENDARY CHARACTERS AND PLACES

CONN OF THE HUNDRED BATTLES

CONN CÉTCHATHACH, or Conn of the Hundred Battles, was a mythical high king of Ireland, fabled as one of the first to rule at Tara. He appeared in several stories in the Fionn Cycle, some of which describe how he was responsible for the death of Cumhall, Fionn's father. Like Connla, his son, Conn had memorable encounters with beings from the Otherworld. The most notable of these was recounted in *Baile in Scail* (The Phantom's Frenzy). Here, the phantom in question was the sun-god, Lugh, who revealed to Conn the number of his descendants who would succeed him as king of Ireland.

THE FAMILY TREE OF CORMAC MAC AIRT,
HIGH KINGS OF IRELAND

CONN OF THE HUNDRED BATTLES
|
ART MAC CUINN (BROTHER OF CONNLA)
|
CORMAC MAC AIRT
|
CAIRBRE LIFECHAIR

CORMAC MAC AIRT

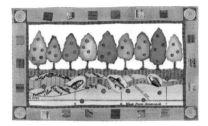

CORMAC WAS RENOWNED as one of the most illustrious high kings of Ireland. He was the grandson of the legendary Conn Cétchathach (Conn of the Hundred Battles) and, even though the Annals state that he ruled from AD 227 to AD 266, he may also have been a mythical figure himself. No historical facts are known about his reign, but a prehistoric structure at Tara is named after him (Cormac's House) and several Celtic tribes claimed him as their ancestor.

In the ancient legends, Cormac featured most heavily in the Fionn Cycle, since his rule coincided with the greatest exploits of the Fianna. He played a fairly peripheral role, although some stories did suggest that Fionn mac Cumhaill served in his royal forces. In addition, there were a few tales that revolved around Cormac himself. One sees his abdication as king after losing an eye, as any physical disability meant an immediate loss of the throne; his son, Cairbre, replaced him. However, the *Echtrae Cormaic* (Adventure of Cormac) that includes the story of the Fairy Branch is the best known of the Cormac stories.

Cú Chulainn

Cú Chulainn, the warrior-hero of Ulster, is the most famous figure in Irish legend. Known as the Hound of Ulster, his exploits form the basis of the most sizeable collection of Irish tales, known as the Ulster Cycle. These focus on an epic narrative called the *Táin Bó Cuailnge* (The Cattle Raid of Cooley) which tells the story of a war between Ulster and Connacht. Maeve, the Queen of Connacht, invades the neighboring kingdom with her army, in order to carry off a magical bull. She does this at a time when the warriors of Ulster are laid low by a curse and are unable to fight. Cú Chulainn alone is immune from this weakness and fights the Connacht army single-handed, sniping with his sling by night and duelling with individual warriors by day.

Cú Chulainn's martial powers are overwhelming. He has been trained by Scáthach, a supernatural Amazonian warrior; he wields an invincible weapon, a spear called the *gae bolga*; and, prior to a fight, he goes into a battle frenzy, which endows him with superhuman strength. With the help of these magical qualities, Cú Chulainn manages to bring about the defeat of Maeve's army.

THE FAMILY TREE OF CÚ CHULAINN

CIAN (CETHERN)
|
LUGH [SUN GOD]
|
CÚ CHULAINN [HERO OF ULSTER]

DIARMAID

Dᴉᴀʀᴍᴀɪᴅ ᴜᴀ Dᴜɪʙʜɴᴇ was a leading member of the Fianna,
appearing in many of the adventures in the Fionn Cycle of legends. He
was skilled as a warrior and a huntsman, although it is as a lover that
he is principally remembered. In the legends, this was emphasized by
the fact that he was fostered by Oenghus, the god of love, and by the
love-spot on his brow.

The most famous of Diarmaid's tales concerns his elopement with
Gráinne. In this, Diarmaid plays Sir Lancelot to Fionn's King Arthur,
carrying off his lord's betrothed. For many years, the couple took
refuge in the countryside and, as a result, many Irish landmarks have
been nicknamed "the bed" or the "bower" of one or other of the lovers.
The Death of Diarmaid is effectively a postscript to the romance.

Fionn mac Cumhaill

Fionn mac Cumhaill was the central hero of the Fionn, or Fenian, Cycle, a collection of legends that revolved around the deeds of Ireland's famous warrior-band, the Fianna. Orphaned at an early age, Fionn acquired the gifts of wisdom and prophecy during his training with Finnegas the Druid, gaining the right to eat the Salmon of Knowledge, which bestowed divine knowledge upon him. While still a youth, he saved Tara – the seat of the high kings – from destruction by a wicked demon, and this won him the leadership of the Fianna. Together with his companions, Fionn then embarked upon a series of colorful adventures, which have been likened to the exploits of King Arthur and the Knights of the Round Table.

Fionn remained a popular legendary figure, endowed with great physical and magical qualities. In the longest of the tales, however, which tells the story of the elopement of Diarmaid and Gráinne, he is shown as a cuckolded husband bitterly seeking revenge against the young lovers. On occasions, Fionn appeared in neighboring cultures, anglicized as Finn McCool or Fingal. As the latter, he was a powerful giant who was deemed responsible for the construction of both the Giant's Causeway in northern Ireland and Fingal's Cave on the island of Staffa.

The Family Tree of Cumhall

Cumhall [leader of the Baiscne]

|

Fionn mac Cumhaill + Sadb [mistress of Fionn]

|

Oisin

122

LIR

O N FIRST READING, the characters in the medieval tale of *The Children of Lir* may seem to be human, but they contain elements of the old Irish gods. These ancient deities were giant beings known as the Tuatha Dé Danaan, or the Danaans. They ruled over Ireland until their defeat by the Milesians, after which they retired to their fairy mounds (or *sidhe*). Lir lived in one of these fairy-dwellings, as its name – Sid Finnachaid – confirms. According to tradition, its site has been linked with Newtown Hamilton, in County Armagh. In spite of his divine origins, however, Lir was not the father of the sea-god, Manannan mac Lir, who appears in *Cormac and the Fairy Branch.*

MORRIGAN

T HE MORRIGAN WAS the most dangerous of all Cú Chulainn's adversaries. In Irish legend, she was one of a trio of war-goddesses, together with Badb and Nemain. She was skilled at shape-shifting, the art of transforming herself from human to animal form, and her favourite guise was that of a crow, picking over corpses on the field of battle. In the *Táin*, she sided with the Connacht army, although she was eventually defeated by Cú Chulainn. Later, she gained her revenge. When the Ulsterman was killed, she alighted on his shoulder in the form of a raven and gloated over his death.

OISIN

OISIN WAS ONE OF Fionn mac Cumhaill's many sons and a leading member of the Fianna. As such, he featured prominently in the tales from the Fionn Cycle. The most important of the early stories were concerned with his supernatural origins (*The Birth of Oisin*) and his visit to the Otherworld. The latter is very similar to *Connla and the Fairy Maiden*, although Oisin did manage to return to his homeland.

In the later legends, Oisin played an increasingly significant role. He was a major figure in the *Acallam na Senorach* (Colloquy of the Elders), a 12th-century text in which Oisin was portrayed as a very old man who had survived long enough to meet St. Patrick. During their meeting, he reminisced about some of his exploits with the Fianna, which had long since disbanded. Later still, in the 18th century, the Scottish poet, James Macpherson, renamed him Ossian and made him the central character in a series of epic poems about the ancient Celtic world. These verses gained immense popularity throughout Europe, becoming one of the seminal texts of the Romantic Movement. Finally, in 1889, W.B. Yeats wrote a narrative poem, entitled *The Wanderings of Oisin*.

OTHERWORLD

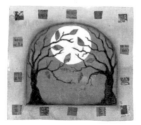

T HE OTHERWORLD was a twilight realm of rebirth, a mystic paradise
that was neither entirely pleasurable nor all painful. Many characters
of the legends, such as Fionn mac Cumhaill, Maeldun and Oisin, pass
through the Otherword or reside there for hundreds of years. It has no
physical location, but on the eve of Samhain, October 31, the gates of
the Otherworld were thought to open, creating a pathway between this
world and the next. This tradition may have been the precursor of
Hallowe'en, as these two festivals share the same date. The Welsh
Otherworld, however, known as Annwn or Avalon, is sometimes
identified with the town of Glastonbury, in Somerset, England.

POOKA

THE POOKA WAS a mischievous, shape-shifting fairy, which figured prominently in Irish folklore. Its origins are much disputed. Over the years, it has been linked with the Welsh pwca, the Norse pukki, the Cornish bucca and the English Puck, although none of these is identical to it. Even within Irish tradition there have been widely differing interpretations of the creature. Some, like Croker, regarded it as a malevolent spirit who spoiled the blackberries after Michaelmas and who, in the guise of a horse, offered dangerous rides to unwary travelers. Indeed, in its most extreme form, Pouk or Puck was occasionally used as a synonym for the Devil. At other times, it could be appeased if a bowl of milk was left out for it at night, just as Cornish fishermen used to leave pieces of bread or fish for the bucca. In the writings of Lady Wilde (*Ancient Legends*, 1887), by contrast, the pooka was a benevolent creature, well disposed towards humanity. More recently, the writer Mary Chase described the invisible rabbit with appeared in her play, *Harvey* (1944) – later immortalized in a film starring James Stewart (1908–2000) as a modern-day pooka.

TARA

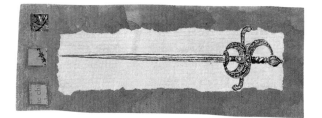

Tara was the ancient seat of the high kings of ancient Ireland. It also served as the base for the Fenians, or Fianna, the mythical band of warriors lead by Fionn mac Cumhaill. Today the hill of Tara exists, close to Newgrange, another sacred site located in the south of Ireland.

Pronunciation Guide

Ailbe *AL-VUH*
Ailil Ochair Aga
   ALIL UKAR AGA
Aine *AW-NYUH*
Aoife *EEF-A*

Bodb *BUD-UV*
Brug na Búinne
   BROO NA BON-YUH

Conn Cétchathach
   KON KAYD-KAH-UK
Cormac mac Airt
   KORMAK MAK ART
Cú Chulainn *KOO HUL-UN*

Diarmaid ua Duibhne
   DEER-MUD OH DIV-NUH
Dubh (the Dark) *DUV*
Dubhan *DUV-UN*

Far Doirche *FAR DUR-KUH*
Fionn mac Cumhaill
   FYUN MAK KOOL

Gae bolga *GAY-BOL-GUH*
Grainne *GRAW-NYA*

Irros Domnann
   IR-ISH DUV-NAN
Iruath *IR-OO-WA*

Loch mac Emonis
   LUK MAK EM-IN-ISH

Maeldun *MAIL-DUN*
Midir (the Proud)
   MI-DIR (THE PROUD)
Milucra *MIL-OO-KRUH*

Mount Muisire
   (MOUNT) MWI-SHI-RUH
Murtagh (Sullivan)
   MUR-TA (SULLIVAN)

Oenghus *AIN-GUS*
Oisin *OSH-EEN*
Owenaght *O-WUH-NAKT*

Sadb *SYVE*
Scáthach *SKA-HUK*
Sceolan *SKYO-LUN*
Sid Finnachaid
   SHEE FIN-UH-KID
Sidhe *SHEE*
Slieve Gullion
   SHLEEV GUL-YUN
St. Gobnait *(SAINT) GUB-NUT*

Tailltin *TAL-TIN*
Tìr na mBeo *TEER NA MYO*

Uar *OOR*